# Mirrors of My Soul

## *A Collection of Everyday Poems*

by

Brenda Morrison Barrett Zeller

DORRANCE PUBLISHING CO
EST. 1920
PITTSBURGH, PENNSYLVANIA 15238

Dorrance Publishing Co
585 Alpha Drive
Suite 103
Pittsburgh, PA 15238
Visit our website at *www.dorrancebookstore.com*

ISBN: 979-8-8868-3023-1
eISBN: 979-8-8868-3888-6

# DEDICATION

Dedicated to my wonderful husband,
Bill Zeller, for including me in all the
great chapters of his life,

And,
to our dear daughter-in-law, Lori R. Barrett,
with gratitude for her time and patience
for adding to the quality of our lives
and her creative contributions to this book.

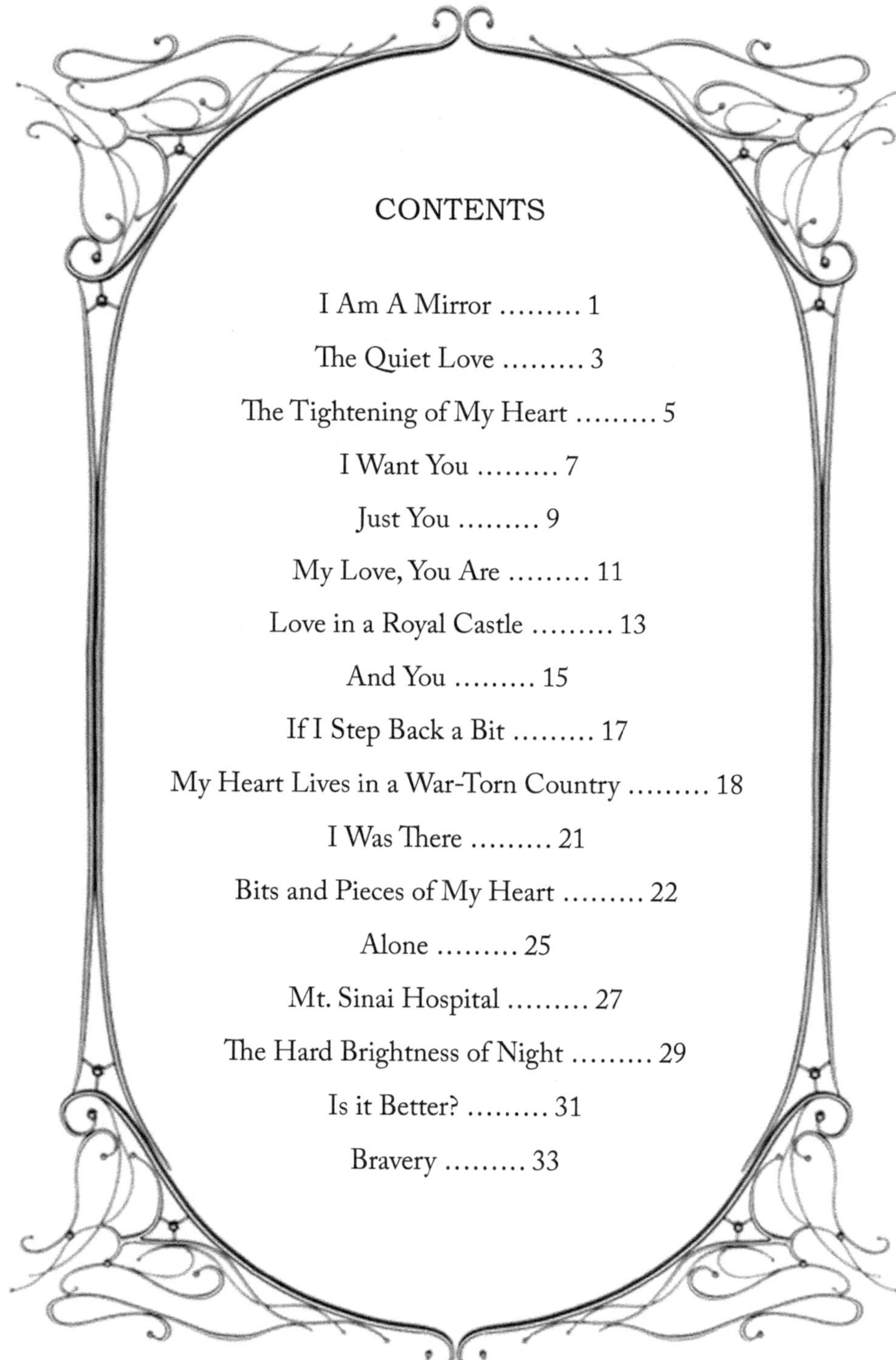

# CONTENTS


I Am A Mirror ......... 1

The Quiet Love ......... 3

The Tightening of My Heart ......... 5

I Want You ......... 7

Just You ......... 9

My Love, You Are ......... 11

Love in a Royal Castle ......... 13

And You ......... 15

If I Step Back a Bit ......... 17

My Heart Lives in a War-Torn Country ......... 18

I Was There ......... 21

Bits and Pieces of My Heart ......... 22

Alone ......... 25

Mt. Sinai Hospital ......... 27

The Hard Brightness of Night ......... 29

Is it Better? ......... 31

Bravery ......... 33

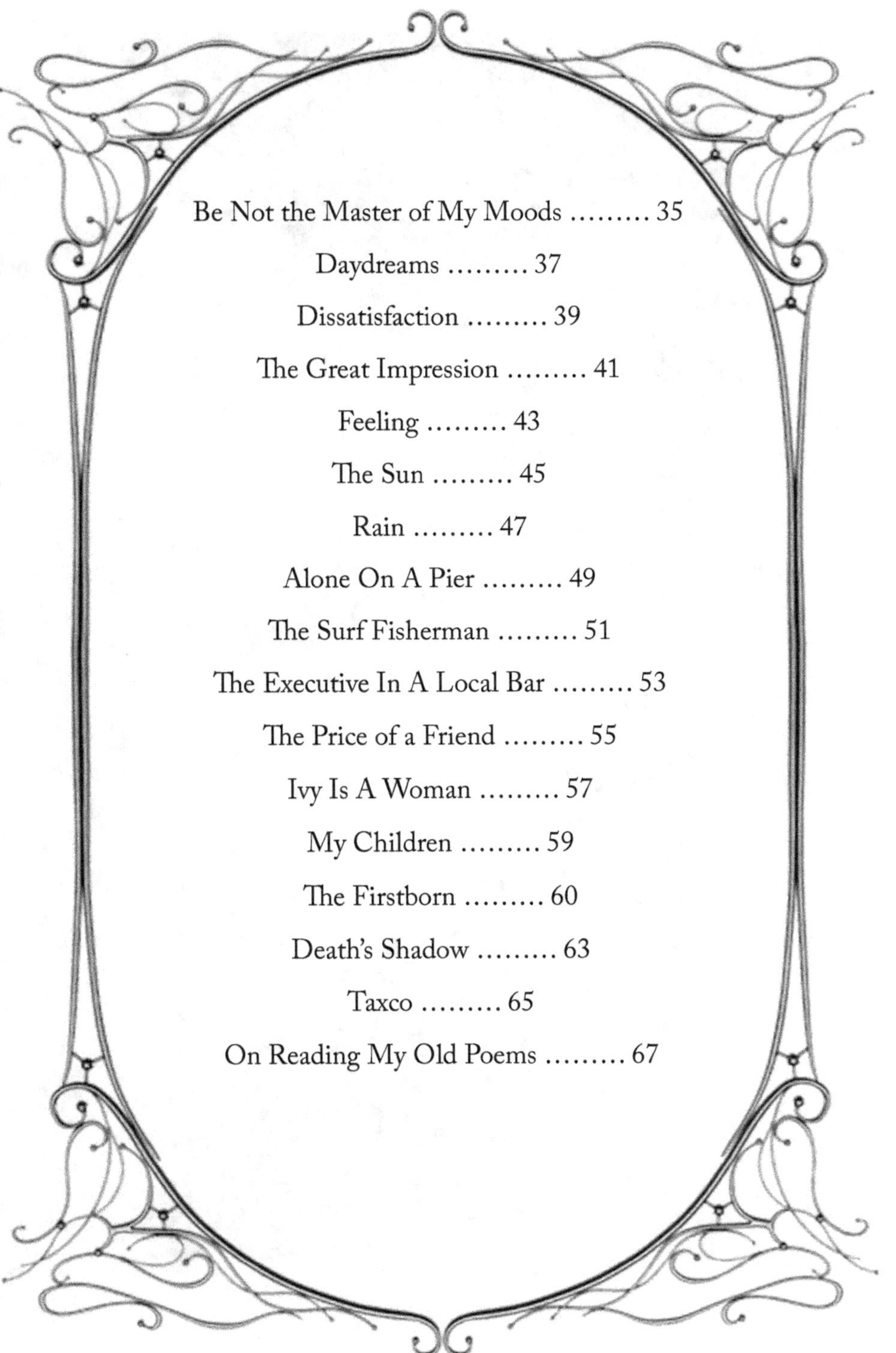


Be Not the Master of My Moods ......... 35

Daydreams ......... 37

Dissatisfaction ......... 39

The Great Impression ......... 41

Feeling ......... 43

The Sun ......... 45

Rain ......... 47

Alone On A Pier ......... 49

The Surf Fisherman ......... 51

The Executive In A Local Bar ......... 53

The Price of a Friend ......... 55

Ivy Is A Woman ......... 57

My Children ......... 59

The Firstborn ......... 60

Death's Shadow ......... 63

Taxco ......... 65

On Reading My Old Poems ......... 67

# I AM A MIRROR

And I, like a mirror
Bounce back all that strikes me.
Reflecting woes of the passerby.
Each tender thought
Strikes my heart and finds sympathy
But is that my own tear I cry?
*Pity poor Polly*
*So laden with care.*
*She could find joy,*
*If only she'd try…*

# THE QUIET LOVE

I am suspicious of the quiet love.
It oozes gently over each part,
Filling each crevice, sealing each break
Silently sliding through my heart.
The quiet love is a gentle one,
Rising from the dark like an early dawn,
Slowly wrapping around your heart
And you never realize it—till it's gone!

# THE TIGHTENING OF MY HEART

That constricting feeling, the tightening of my heart,
The warm feeling, lying just below the skin,
That, my darling, is how I feel when we meet, when we part.
So many wonderfully happy things I can't keep in.
I want to love you, be with you, to kiss you.
I look at a leaf, your face peeks out between the veins.
I hear the catch in your voice on the phone; I miss you.
I pass a window and see—your smile reflected in the panes.
There's so little I can give to you, only my thoughts for you.

# I WANT YOU

I want to know you, to love you, to care
To think about you during my waking hours,
Feel your closeness in the night,
When the shadows roll through my room.
I want to wrap my love around you,
Close enough when the strange unhappinesses
Steal your lightheartedness, my love is there,
A diligent soldier dispelling the gloom
Worry about you, My Love? Of course!
The sad things, that line your face,
Become my past and present too.
The good things too are there to share.
My love does not demand equal measure,
Doling out inch for inch returned.
My love cannot face a yardstick,
There are none of length to compare.
I want to be your strength in time of depression,
Just as I draw from your solidity.
I shall garner each bit of joy, happiness, serenity,
My store shall have but one key.

# JUST YOU

I'll find a way,
Someday, one way—
To tell you—just you,
Why none but you will do.
I may not use words sublime
Perfected by lovers through time.
But if it is by words that I choose,
T'will be Truth—no plot, no ruse!
And if I find a Force is best,
What shall I do to meet this test?
I could scale an imposing mountain with skill,
T'would awe the world, but a mountain is just a hill.
Or perhaps I should try to be right in my actions
Orderly, austere, absolutely impervious to distraction.
Oh, I could make such grand promises and resolutions!
But how formidable—to love such an institution
But each method seems too small,
An understatement that seems to fall
Too short. Each way too dramatic
For such as me who is quietly ecstatic.
——————— and so this lament shall continue
until I find a way
someday, one way, to say,
why none but you will do!

# MY LOVE, YOU ARE

You are the imagination of a child
Run rampant through the untrodden field.
You are that unseen mercurial knack
Eluding all restraints, the world may wield.
You are the free-floating clouds that
Scamper across the strips of blue above.
You are soundless depth of a mirrored pond
Above all, you are—My Love.

# LOVE IN A ROYAL CASTLE

We counted our pennies and added
Yours and mine to the stack
Wonderful days of love
Wish that they were back.
Could anything be better than
Those hamburgers and Coke?
No chateaubriand could compare
Simply because we were broke!

# AND YOU

And you, you stepped through the gate
That once closed around my heart
And walked out,
Taking nothing.
In you I reached, I hoped, I planned.
That bit of eagerness restored me
I forgot all life is about
In you I was a child again.

# IF I STEP BACK A BIT

And if I step back a bit,
It is not to escape you,
But only time's old habit,
To better look anew.
Who can say yet, what you are to me,
Or I to you, nothing more than
Another day, another time to be.
To be the only, or yet another man?
The faint stirrings of simple joy
Tug at the well-wrapped heart.
I clutch the shreds that will not cloy
But race each other to be apart.

# MY HEART LIVES IN A WAR-TORN COUNTRY

My heart lives in war-torn country
Filled with acrimony and hate
It used to be quite different
Full of love that couldn't wait.
My heart survives in a precarious land
Bombarded with recrimination and blame
Where love once freely dwelled
His insecurity has dimmed the flame.
I tiptoe through my daily life
Careful not to step on a latent bomb
That sets my partner's tirades flowing
Blowing and destroying the calm.
Where once his delight was to count my glories
Reveling in my talents and happy ways
Now he corrupts them to sad stories
Furiously expanding my simple flaws.
How does my heart beat in this sad country?
The way consists of quiet measure,
Beat by beat of his good parts
I count the joys in him I treasure.
I am a stranger in this bombarded land
My heart waits silently strong
Questioning the source of such derision
Wondering where his thoughts went wrong.

Is this a natural progression
Of some strange and malevolent disease
Or has he turned to some dark corner
My soul wonders how to please.
My heart was once an open door
In this strange war-like land
Now my heart slowly closes
Knowing its limits able to stand.
My heart wanders through this dark land
Verbal Abuse is its name
It is a cowardly adversary
Biting and kicking in secret shame.
It leaves no marks, no visible scar
None to know or suspect,
Only hurt left to mar,
My memories lost to self-respect.
His need for me fanned the fires
Of Flames long forgotten in memory
Of love and abandonment and pain
Mutual need should be our treasury.
Words of anger
Tears of pain
Hit my heart like falling rain
Scattering, shattering Love as it goes.

# I WAS THERE

I was there just in front of you
The day our first words were spoken.
Your heart full of ghosts and shadows,
I with my heart wide open.
I was there—just beside you
As we romped our romance through.
The ghosts gathered tight around,
I lagged beside—you never knew!
I was there—just behind you,
Through fantasies we'd wander.
The ghosts stepped on their pedestals.
I slowly stopped to ponder.
I was NOT there—near you.
You little seemed to note,
You never really saw me,
Or heard the songs we wrote.
And now I'm there beside him,
Some other time and place,
A part of my heart is sad,
I no longer see your face.

# BITS AND PIECES OF MY HEART

Bits and pieces of my heart
Is all you wanted from the start
Your life full with another
No room at all for any other.
At 20 I was young
A frightened heart on the run
I wanted someone to take all
My bits and pieces, large and small
And so, we each went our way
Two hearts wandering far astray
Friendship only kept its tender vow
To other loves our hearts did bow.
At 40 our hearts returned
To the love we left adjourned
But still, bits and pieces alone
Were all your heart would condone.
And Friendship again was all we spared
And empty space, for love unshared.
At 60 two hearts spoke again
Love for us we knew not when
A love not strong enough to last
Our faint dream of love long past.
Another lady graced your life
Who truly should have been your wife.
My heart breaks for her, my friend
Life's best gift, lost in the end.
My heart has finally found its mate
Someone who bits and pieced my fate
But still we are entwined
A Friendship death cannot unbind.

We said Goodbye, my love, long ago
But now my heart's hardest blow
Is to know this is the true end
And say Goodbye, my love, my friend.

# ALONE

The phone—How often I awaited its ring.
That longed-for jangling of noise
...Someone does care.
My senses leap and bound
Tumbling over one another
In their unfounded eagerness
Logic tells me there was no sound.
...You are not there.

# MT. SINAI HOSPITAL

Faraway windows, divided four-square
Surrounded by the murk of night.
A single light stationed here and there,
Through my window—my boundaries of sight.
The sad slapping of rainy water
Hitting my chords with each fall.
Surely, I am Proserpine's daughter,
Six months of light and dark in all.
Six months of waiting for my life,
To rise and fall with each tide,
But now, only lying like a tin soldier
That some child should return to life.
Some sweet child shall spy me
And hug me to his breast,
And with his kiss awaken me,
From my long and dreary rest.

# THE HARD BRIGHTNESS OF NIGHT

The Frightening Darkness of day.
The Hard Brightness of night,
These are my masters,
And I fear.
The day creeps into my soul,
Prying, pushing, missing nothing.
As a strong, black shadow creeps over the land,
Covering, consuming all that is near
The Night, the Night's brittle light is a cover,
A blending agent that lulls its victim,
Gloss on the surface, hiding the inner man,
Leading him to believe that here is retreat.
Each phase passes,
The toll is taken,
Meted out in my emotional exhaustion,
And still, I fear.

# IS IT BETTER?

Is it better that:
The things I do in haste
Perhaps undo all done by time
The days of emotional waste.
Or am I, too, a fool sublime?

    *Brenda Morrison Barrett Zeller*

# BRAVERY

Ride the horse!
The big white charger.
The plains of life feel his step.
Sit proud and high.
Seat steady and firm.
The following herd awaits the fallen.

# BE NOT THE MASTER OF MY MOODS

Though my mood may change
Fret not, long not for the set.
Be not the master of my mood,
But companion, watcher, or better yet...
Come along with me as I wander
Through a black abysmal pass
Shaking the mud from my feet,
Treading the cool green grass.
The captive bird only breaks his wings, flailing
in his bound.
Aback!—See the beauty of his soft flight from
sky to ground.

# DAYDREAMS

There was a dark and dreary time.
My thoughts were dismal and gray.
Wild phantoms inhabited my nights,
Worse yet, **REALITY** was my day.
I put aside my old friend, Daydreams.
I had no time for such luxury,
And beamed thoughts on my failures,
A task of infinite drudgery.

# DISSATISFACTION

Dissatisfaction slides o'er me
Lulling and dulling my brain
Wrapping my thoughts in dust
Blackness leaving its stain.

# THE GREAT IMPRESSION

A word is uttered, a sentence said,
Truth colored to every shade.
Thoughts exchanged, communicated,
Groundwork for the Great Impression laid!
This facade so woven, behind which to hide,
How often traps its creator
Enmeshing him, snaring him, leaving him tied
To a fictional life—a selfish master!

# FEELING

A feeling is meant to be enjoyed,
An emotion, cherished in a tender heart.
None are meant to be lightly aired
Nor dissected—brutally torn apart.
But to appreciate a few words,
To live each feeling—to understand each thought
To realize the significance of minute emotions,
A lesson which can be learned, seldom taught.
The hardest thing in this world to do,
Is to realize the infinite futility
Attempting to impart our deepest feelings
To others, without regard for humility.
Some may at one time or another
Feel as we do and be empathetic,
But to express our feeling to one unaffected,
Takes the legerdemain of a verbal trick.

44    *Brenda Morrison Barrett Zeller*

# THE SUN

The Sun
Warms, wraps itself
Around the Earth,
Touching each bit of land.
It gently nudges the sleeping.
Blooms and pulls the dozing leaf
Awake into bright expectancy...
The fingers of God's hand.
How capriciously it slides
Across the Rosamund-like pool,
The silver streamers of light
Pushing back the black-blanketed blue.
At last, tired from its ancient charge,
It jettisons its last bit of life
And in one final burst makes
Its promise of a tomorrow anew.

# RAIN

The droplets fall
Each racing to be the first
To touch the ground.
Breaking free from the cloud
That mothered them, they
Start their search around.
Each one's trip begins.
What wonders to witness?
What unknown awaits them.
Downward, plunging
Twisting, turning, lunging.
Falling on some lithe stem.
The hungry dirt grasps
Each bit of dew and asks
All—their life—their death.
At last, the end.
The ultimate,
The Earth.

   *Brenda Morrison Barrett Zeller*

# ALONE ON A PIER

And I tried to tell you just how I felt,
That pale, cool night on the pier,
To tell you how safe and warm I was,
How happy and free from fear.
And I thought,
But didn't say:
"The distant noise of the city,
Cannot reach us,
Touch us,
Here."
You smiled at me,
In your soft way:
"Such is serenity—
Life's belief,
Sweet relief,
You are near."

# THE SURF FISHERMAN

Water, lapping about my feet
Warm and clean and sweet.
Water, bathe away my care
Water, help me breathe fresh air.
Those nibbling kisses on my toes
Each tiny wave comes and goes,
Tickling and tingling my skin,
Till even glum I must grin.
Water, where have you been?
Would that I could only jump in,
Shedding my fishing rod and clothes,
On the bank with all my woes.

# THE EXECUTIVE IN A LOCAL BAR

And there he sits—The Executive.
Broad smile crossing his corpulent face,
Back slapping, hand pumping,
Trying to maintain the social pace.
Carefully creased suit,
Over initialed shirt draped,
Tie enclosing chubby neck,
Hat deliberately shaped.
His great accomplishments
Intoned to the room at large.
But does this tycoon have cash?
Oh, no—with him it is "Charge."
Must he at such length expound
Over long and loudly talk.
To cover up that telltale sound
Of his two dimes, jingling with his walk!

# PRICE OF A FRIEND

There is a price on every phase of life
Those who enjoy must be prepared to spend
No passing fancy, no momentary gain
Ever too high for a friend.
So, measure any small token
Each action not explained
Lest the final result be ruined
Vows of a friend not easily broken.

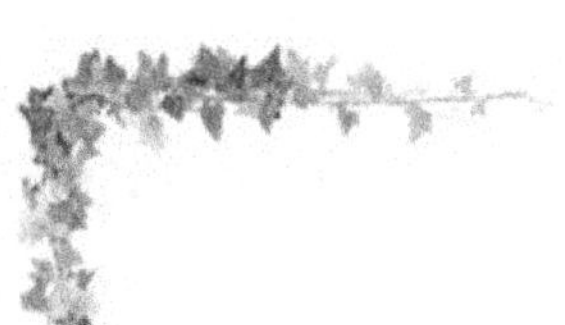

# IVY IS A WOMAN

The Poison Ivy vine grows
Sturdy, strong, deceptive in beauty.
The cool warmth of her skin,
Soft to the touch, stroked soothingly.
Bright red lips has she,
Round globules of splashy color
Attracting the curious eyes
Of children, marveling her allure.
Fed by the sun of attention,
A love-starved woman grows
Covering, crowding, choking the life
Away from all others existing close.
At last! The ultimate! The coveted ground won,
At a price too high to atone.
The battle won—none left to be admired but Ivy,
And mockingly—none left to behold. She is alone!

# MY CHILDREN

Before you,
Life was:
Champagne at noon
Velvet brocade
A passing parade
A haunting tune.
Life anew,
Good because:
I'd never trade
Baby's spoon
Cool lemonade,
A mother's croon.
Cocktail glasses tinkling,
Gay, exciting people.
Bright lights, marquees twinkling.
And now my greatest treat
Is kissing baby's chubby feet.

# THE FIRSTBORN

I sit with you, my love, my little girl
Your chair raised high to meet the world
Bright eyes peering from under brown curl
Fingers exploring, toes tightly curled.
Safe in your bunny-print sleeper
With a million new things to explore
So safe, with love as your keeper
How glad we are to adore.
Outside the world is uncertain
Crises threaten all peace.
But you merely yank on the curtain
And cheerfully make a new crease.
So much for you to learn
So many happenings to meet
So many bridges to burn
So many wonders to greet.
I'd like to wrap up all life for you
In a huge box with a frilly bow,
Keep you from making errors anew
And have all life fresh as you go.

But the joy of living is discovery
Each new thing a great wonder
The bliss of mistake is recovery,
So on, my love, you must blunder.
You're never alone no matter how sad
No matter how hard the task
We've been through it too, the good the bad,
Maybe we can help, just ask.
We've a special love for you
This gray ol' world can never touch.
You've made our lives and hearts anew
Is it enough to say, "We love you so much"?

# DEATH'S SHADOW

Sad thoughts come when you feel death's shadow
Chilling your back!
You think of unfinished projects,
You know your lack!
Who will care for your loved ones,
Be there with their needs,
And tell the babe of marvelous things,
And sow Wonderment's seeds.

# TAXCO

The faint shimmering of haze
Standing on tiptoe, stretching from the ground,
Trying vainly to climb up to the heaven
Cattle nuzzling the grass as they graze,
The happy quiver of a sweet bud, found
The ancient church-bells striking seven
This, the country viewed from TAXCO!
Winding, twisting, the rough-smooth cobbles
Touch each other to form a way
To lure the stubborn, sleepy mules.
Here no need of great restriction or hobbles
Here no great division of time and day
Here only to seek the quiet, the cool
This smoldering part of MEXICO!
The house gnaws its way into the hollow of a hill
The artist layers his thoughts on canvas,
Blending in each stroke the warm body of the sun
The flowers race to be the first to spill
Bright red blossoms on each roof, each crevice.
This, then tumbling into the final One—
All this, the love, the warmth of TAXCO!

# ON READING MY OLD POEMS

As I sit here watching my parade of thought
Kaleidoscope in front of my eyes—
A smile marks my lips and I realize
That all I thought I was—I'm not.
My self-reflection changed each day.
I thought I was a cynic with a soul—
Yet again, a starlet without a role.
All these passed and none would stay.
And in another, my heart was dark.
Blackness curled its edges tight,
Squeezing me in its perpetual night.
Hope was but a faint-remembered spark.
And now, my life has come full swing.
The soul within me long suppressed
No longer will lie fallow
Little caring for what life can bring.